I Don't Have Time To Write

And Other Lies Writers Tell Ourselves

Author Success Foundations Book 7

by

Christopher di Armani

Copyright © 2018 Christopher di Armani

All rights reserved.

ISBN-13: 978-1988938134

Editor: Nicolas Johnson

Published By:
Botanie Valley Productions Inc.
PO Box 507
Lytton, BC V0K 1Z0
http://BotanieValleyProductions.com

Dedication

This book is dedicated to my sweet and loving wife Lynda. Without her unwavering support none of this would be possible.

Acknowledgments

Without the assistance of my editor, Nicolas Johnson, I can't imagine how this book would read. He tears my words apart from every conceivable angle, then offers thoughtful and constructive criticism on how best to fix the destruction at our feet. I thank God for Nicolas Johnson and his talents, daily.

#EditorsMatter

Feedback Loop

I also wish to express my heartfelt gratitude to the following individuals who took time from their own busy lives to critique this manuscript. Their willingness to assist a total stranger humbles me.

Kim Steadman (KimSteadman.com)
Sharilee Swaity (Facebook.com/Sharilee.Swaity)

Table of Contents

Foreword	1
I Don't Have Time to Write	3
I Suffer From Writer's Block	13
My First Draft Must Be Perfect	23
I'll Remember That Great Idea	27
Outlines Stifle My Creativity	29
I Don't Need A Professional Editor	35
I'm Not Talented Enough To Be A Writer	37
One Last Thing	38
About The Author	39
Books by Christopher di Armani	40
Endnotes	46

Foreword

In this installment of the Author Success Foundations series, I dissect seven lies writers tell ourselves and shine the light of truth upon each one.

Every falsehood obscures a truth we refuse to confront. The job of a writer, any writer, is to face our fears head on, protected by the body armor of honesty and integrity. Only then does the brilliance we etch on the page shine bright for the world to see.

Each delusion corrodes holes in our armor, holes the insidious demons of worry, self-doubt, procrastination and perfectionism slip through to poison us.

The Author Success Foundations series provides the tools and materials to patch those holes, to reinforce and strengthen our armor. The day of battle is here, and we must march ever forward. If we stop, even for a moment, our words shrink under the oppressive heat of our fears and we fail.

Step inside.

Face your fears.

Show these pathetic demons you cannot be cowed.

Own your internal dialogue and reshape it into a powerful engine, then use that power to drive down Publication Highway.

I Don't Have Time To Write, and Other Lies

Chapter 1

I Don't Have Time To Write

All Writers Are Liars

Storytelling is the stuff of dreams, of fantasy and imagination. We invoke our lies to explain fundamental truths to our readers.

Twisting the truth is our job, our calling even, so it's no surprise to learn we deceive ourselves far more than our readers. The depths we plumb to fool ourselves is surpassed only by the height of our self-deception.

Let's face the cold, hard truth.

The only person who loses when we lie to ourselves is us.

When we tell ourselves we don't have time to write, or writing is difficult, or I'll just do it later, what we're really saying is this:

We don't value writing.

That's a problem. If we don't value writing, we will never make the hard choices necessary to put our manuscript first. We will find a way to put other pursuits ahead of it, fun but unimportant folly that wastes our precious time and guarantees we never finish our book.

Fortunately, there is a simple solution.

"The art of writing is the art of applying the seat of the pants to the seat of the chair."

— Mary Heaton Vorse

I Don't Have Time to Write

Let's tackle the biggest lie first.

I don't have time to write.

Garbage.

Each day, you possess one thousand, four hundred and forty precious minutes. You cannot save them for tomorrow. You cannot replenish your stock. You can only invest those minutes wisely today, in the hopes of greater returns tomorrow.

Whether you spend your time sensibly or not, the choice is yours. The choice is always yours.

You control your direction by the decisions you make. Forward progress is inevitable, unstoppable and unavoidable, but will you move forward toward success or failure?

Jim Rohn says you cannot make progress if you don't make decisions. Brian Tracy says you either make excuses or make progress. Essentially, Rohn and Tracy make the same point. You must make a conscious choice to move forward toward success. Anything less dooms you to failure.

Nobody has time to write. Nobody finds the time to write either. You must make the time. You must make a choice to advance your career, not deepen your failure.

The real question you must ask yourself is not, "How do I find more time to write?"

The real question is

"What am I willing to give up to make more time for writing each day?"

Your honest answer to this question drives you toward your finished manuscript faster than any other choice you make.

It's okay, I'll write tomorrow

It's okay if I don't write today. I will write tomorrow. I know I can make up the time.

No, it is *not* okay if you don't write today. If you choose not to write today, you cannot make up your lost ground tomorrow.

Sure, you can choose to spend more of tomorrow's precious time on it, but promising to do tomorrow what you know you should do today is a recipe for one thing, and it's not a finished manuscript.

Procrastination drops a boat anchor and halts your progress. When you tell yourself it's okay, you'll write tomorrow instead, you allow fear to rule your life.

Procrastination is also a sign of laziness, of your lack of focus, lack of determination and lack of self-discipline.

The neon sign of procrastination flashes the truth over your head for the world to see - you don't value writing. It's not important.

If it was, you would make a different choice.

Let me give you an example from my own life. This morning I received bad news. Sure, I expected the news, but it shook me, nonetheless. It rattled my cage and dumped me out of my comfortable mindset into a cold bucket of self-doubt and self-recrimination. I don't write well when I lack confidence or beat myself up for the actions beyond my control.

Life happens. Good news happens. Bad news happens, too. The proof you take writing seriously is in your actions, when you write every day, regardless of what "good" or "bad" news lands on your doorstep.

The only way any writer finishes their book is to do the work required.

Despite how my day started, I continue to work on this book. I don't stop working because it is inconvenient or I don't feel like it.

Writers persevere in the face of setbacks. We don't allow them to control us.

Writing Is Hard

I don't know if we say writing is hard to justify ourselves to others, or because we truly believe it. Maybe it's both.

Mark Twain said, "The secret of getting ahead is getting started. The secret of getting started is breaking your complex, overwhelming tasks into small manageable tasks, and then starting on the first one."

Precisely.

Here's my truth.

Writing is easy. Getting started is my nightmare.

This is the nut I must crack every day:
1. Plant my butt in the chair each morning.
2. Turn on my computer.
3. Make the decision to write.
4. Follow my good decision with the action required, and write.

Writing is never difficult. The moment I begin, words flow like water. My issue is part procrastination, part indecision, and part lack of knowledge of what I must write. These are my primary excuses - and they are excuses.

To get around my inherent desire to fritter my time away, I wrote a little computer program to put me under the pressure of a deadline. It's a Pomodoro writing timer. Nothing fancy. On my worst days, I set the timer for five minutes, then lie to myself.

Just write for five lousy minutes, then quit. No problem.

A strange thing happens in my brain the moment I click the start button. As soon as I see the timer's hand tick off the seconds, I feel the pressure to write. It doesn't matter that the deadline is completely artificial. It's still a deadline, and my brain is wired to meet deadlines.

It's the strangest experience as the pressure wells up inside me. It doesn't go away, either, until I pound on the keyboard. The moment I begin, the pressure releases, because I finally started to do what I am supposed to do: write.

Often, the timer startles me when it expires. In those few short minutes, I became so engrossed in my story I forgot I started the timer. It did its job. It got me off my lazy butt. Awesome.

If you describe yourself as a project-oriented person, and most writers are, I suggest you try my timer technique and see if it works for you. If your brain is wired to meet deadlines, like mine, you now have a new tool in your writer's toolbox. Use it to jump-start your writing session.

But Writing is Difficult

Your brain is the world's greatest supercomputer. Like all computers, it follows the instructions given to it perfectly, every single time. If you think writing is hard, rewrite your code. Tell yourself writing is easy. Repeat the mantra for thirty seconds. Do this every day for a month and marvel at the transformation of your beliefs.

Can you see why this is a problem for me? I said writing is easy but getting started is hard. Why would I want to reinforce failure with this self-destructive belief? I don't. I want to change it. I can change it. All it takes is for me to recode my beliefs.

Yes, I make it sound so easy. It's simple. If it was easy, everyone would do it.

Reprogramming a computer is hard work. It's also essential work. Recoding my mind is a daily process, reinforced by my self-discipline and dedication. Yeah, I say this like self-discipline and dedication are easy, too. I get it.

Simple, not easy.

Back to my own messed-up internal programming. Getting started is not difficult. It's just as easy as the actual writing, but my own sick belief still causes me trouble. My job is to rewrite the code - to turn my negative belief into a positive statement.

Getting started to write is easier than writing.

I already believe writing is easy, so if I tell my brain getting started is even easier, my days should become more productive in no time.

This is my daily challenge. If it's yours too, start with the belief writing is easy. Set a timer, sit down in your chair and write, even if it's for five lousy minutes. The beauty of this trick is, for me, once I begin I don't want to stop. Still, I do need a kick in the butt to get me started. For a guy who loves writing as much as I do, isn't that a ridiculous thought? Hey, I never said my mind makes sense. I only said I can reprogram it to force more words out each day.

"Confront the page that taunts you with its whiteness. Face your enemy and fill it with words. You are bigger and stronger than a piece of paper."

— Fennel Hudson

I'll Just Check Facebook First

I'll start writing as soon as I check Facebook.

No, you won't. You'll be stuck in Facebook's time-sucking vortex for the next hour, probably two. The same goes for all the other social media websites where you squander your precious writing time.

Nothing on Facebook or any other social media platform is as important as writing. Nothing. It can all wait until you finish writing.

At most, you put it off for what? Two or three hours? Anything can wait for two or three hours. *Anything.*

The other problem with social media is its negative impact on your mental state. The massive influx of sensory input, both visual and audio, bombards your mind and destroys any chance of a calm and centered mind.

I write best when my mind is calm and focused on the task at hand. You may be able to write well after bombarding your mind with thousands of random thoughts, but I suggest you are in the extreme minority. If I wanted to be blunt, I would suggest you're lying to yourself.

Do yourself a favour. Leave Facebook, Twitter, Snapchat and all those other shiny toys alone until after you're done writing for the day.

Make it a game. Turn social media into your reward when you meet your day's word count. Reward yourself with five minutes on Facebook for every 500 words you write. Better yet, reward yourself after 1,000 words hit the page.

Make it an incentive for a job well done. You'll be more focused and write more in less time every day - all because you postponed your social media fix for a few hours.

You say you want to write a book.

Prove it.

Write.

Play with social media when you're done.

I'll Write After The Next Episode of...

No, you won't. I assure you, from personal experience, the last episode of the season will end before you stop. Only when your eyes are so bloodshot you can no longer see, and so exhausted you cannot keep your eyes open, will you turn off the TV and fall into bed.

As enjoyable as the television show may be, you managed to waste your entire evening with the stupid box, instead of writing another chapter of your book.

As I suggested with social media, turn your television into a reward for writing. Only after you achieve your target word count do you receive the prize.

If you don't achieve your word count, no television. You must suffer the consequences for failure, as well as reap the rewards of success.

Hold yourself accountable. Yes, every single day.

I'll Try To Write Today

I'll try to write today.

This lie means you won't write a single word. You will find something else to fill up your time until it's too late. Then you will lie to yourself again and tell yourself you will write tomorrow, instead.

Yoda said it best when he admonished Luke Skywalker.

"Do. Or do not. There is no try."

Yoda was right. You cannot try to do anything. You either do it or you don't.

Write today or don't. Either way, stop lying to yourself about it. Take responsibility for your decision and your action or, in case you choose not to write it all, your inaction. Either choice is fine so long as you take responsibility for it, so long as you make the conscious choice not to write. Don't slough it off, saying you'll try a little later. You won't, and you know it. This particular rabbit hole has trapped you far too many times already.

Do you want to write today?

Make an appointment with yourself and then keep the appointment. Schedule it on your day timer or set a reminder on your phone. When the reminder pops up, honor your commitment. Sit down at your computer and write.

Find a reward to motivate yourself. Find one thing you want to do and, if you meet your goal, fantastic, do it. If you don't achieve your target word count or worse, you do not write at all, withhold the treat.

Be merciless. Make yourself accountable and honor your commitments.

We writers are slow learners. It's sad. Writing is what we do. In a large part, it's who we are and yet we make every excuse in the book to avoid doing the thing we love most.

Sounds like pure insanity to me.

Just do it.

Leave the excuses and rationalizations for the slacker down the street.

I'll Write When I Have More Time

I don't have time today. I'll write tomorrow, when I have more time.

You will never have more time. Grab a hammer off the desk and smash yourself in the forehead with it, right now. You need to get this through your thick skull, like I need to get it through mine.

I always have time to write. Unfortunately, I choose not to write far too often.

Action is proof of commitment. A commitment without action is nothing more than pretty words designed to make failure acceptable. Failure is not an option, not if you're a writer.

As I mentioned earlier, I receive the gift of one thousand four hundred and forty minutes every single day. I, alone, decide how to spend those priceless and irreplaceable gems. Once spent, they are gone forever so I better choose wisely.

The *I don't have time to write* lie is the hallmark of someone who does not make writing a priority in their life.

Is your finished book important? Be honest. If the answer is yes, your next decision is simple. What activity will you give up or do less often to make time to write? An hour of television? The time you fritter away on social media? Another of the many time-wasting activities you enjoy?

If finishing your book is essential to your happiness, you will behave accordingly. You will stop lying to yourself.

You will schedule an appointment with yourself every day, time you set aside to write and nothing else, and you will keep the appointment.

"Journalist: a person without any ideas but with an ability to express them; a writer whose skill is improved by a deadline: the more time he has, the worse he writes."

— Karl Kraus

Finishing My Manuscript is So Hard

Finishing my book is so hard.

Um, yeah. Of course it is. I'm shocked you think it could be any other way.

When literary giant Ernest Hemingway says, "The hard part about writing a novel is finishing it," what makes you think it will be easier for you?

You are not alone. Not by a long shot.

Do what Hemingway did. Sit down and write.

"I went for years not finishing anything. Because, of course, when you finish something you can be judged," said Erica Jong.

Put your fear aside and write.

Don't worry. All your anxiety, fear, procrastination and other glorious horrors await your return. Plus, they know where to find you.

If you're lucky, really lucky, you will finish your manuscript before those wretched little monkeys jump on your back and flay your self-discipline.

"Whatever it takes to finish things, finish. You will learn more from a glorious failure than you ever will from something you never finished."

— Neil Gaiman

I Don't Have Time To Write, and Other Lies

Chapter 2

I Suffer From Writer's Block

Disease, Condition, Malady or Something More Sinister?

"Writer's block is just another name for fear."
— Jacob Nordby

Wikipedia[1] defines writer's block as *a condition, primarily associated with writing, in which an author loses the ability to produce new work or experiences a creative slowdown. The condition ranges in difficulty from coming up with original ideas to being unable to produce a work for years.*

Writer's block is a condition. Sounds so mild, doesn't it? A condition is hardly even a thing.

Oh, we writers know better. It's a thing, all right, and not a mild thing either. It's bloody serious!

Webster's Dictionary[2] defines writer's block as *the problem of not being able to think of something to write about or not being able to finish writing a story, poem, etc. and a psychological inhibition preventing a writer from proceeding with a piece.*

The idea I'm not being able to think of something to write about doesn't thrill me.

If this makes me sound like a whiny little bitch, *psychological inhibition preventing the writer from proceeding* is far worse. It says I manufacture the problem in my head - the writer's version of hypochondriac.

I am not some crazed neurotic. I'm a *writer*.

Dictionary.com[3] defines writer's block as a *temporary condition in which a writer finds it impossible to proceed with the writing of a novel, play, or other work*.

I can't speak for you but, at times, it doesn't feel so temporary to me. And they used that nasty word "condition" again, too. Not a fan.

Urban Dictionary[4] defines writer's block as a *psychological inability to begin or continue work on a piece of writing*.

Now we're getting somewhere. It's a psychological inability. That's a thing for sure. I'd bet money on it. Even better, it's not my fault I can't write. I'm psychologically unable.

I don't suffer this psychological inability alone. I'm surrounded by the most brilliant authors of all time, including Leo Tolstoy, Virginia Woolf, F. Scott Fitzgerald, Charles M. Schultz, Katherine Mansfield, and Joseph Conrad, to name but a few. They all suffered from this malady, terrorized by the same demon you and I face each day.

Do their confessions of powerlessness give you hope?

They shouldn't.

News Flash!

I can't write today. I have writer's block.

News Flash: Writer's block is an even bigger lie than telling yourself you don't have time to write.

Writer's block is a bigger lie than telling yourself you don't have time to write. The single greatest gift you can give yourself is the knowledge writer's block does not exist. It's a fallacy; a stupid notion invented by a brilliant writer to explain to his irate boss why he missed his deadline.

Unfortunately, his editor bought into the lie and a whole subculture of writer's maladies sprang to life.

Writer's block is procrastination on steroids. Writer's block is you making the conscious choice not to do your job.

It's your flat-out refusal to write.

I love Oscar Wilde's quote.

> "I don't believe in it (writer's block). All writing is difficult. The most you can hope for is a day when it goes reasonably easily. Plumbers don't get plumber's block, and doctors don't get doctor's block; why should writers be the only profession that gives a special name to the difficulty of working, and then expect sympathy for it?"

Writer's block is a manufactured malady. It is a horrendous deception foisted upon writers all too willing to believe a lie to validate their desire to procrastinate.

Writer's block excuses our failure to focus, our failure to apply diligence and self-discipline.

Does this sound harsh? If so, I suggest you take a long, hard look in the mirror and find out which button I smashed with my hammer. Replace it with a non-faulty version.

Confront yourself, at every opportunity, to ensure you don't live in delusion. Apply self-discipline, keep the appointment with your keyboard and write.

Or will you cling to the misguided belief your manuscript will write itself?

"There's no such thing as writer's block. That was invented by people in California who couldn't write."

— Terry Pratchett

I Need Inspiration to Write

"Do not wait to strike till the iron is hot; but make it hot by striking."

— William B. Sprague

Another common manifestation of the writer's block deception is, "I can't write unless I'm inspired."

Peter DeVries says, "I only write when I'm inspired, and I see to it that I'm inspired at nine o'clock every morning."

Inspiration is for amateurs.

Professionals get down to work.

Philip Pullman takes it a step farther, with bonus points for attitude.

> "Writer's block…a lot of howling nonsense would be avoided if, in every sentence containing the word WRITER, that word was taken out and the word PLUMBER substituted; and the result examined for the sense it makes. Do plumbers get plumber's block? What would you think of a plumber who used that as an excuse not to do any work that day?
>
> The fact is that writing is hard work, and sometimes you don't want to do it, and you can't think of what to write next, and you're fed up with the whole damn business. Do you think plumbers don't feel like that about their work from time to time? Of course there will be days when the stuff is not flowing freely. What you do then is MAKE IT UP.
>
> I like the reply of the composer Shostakovich to a student who complained that he couldn't find a theme for his second movement. 'Never mind the theme! Just write the movement!' he said.
>
> Writer's block is a condition that affects amateurs and people who aren't serious about writing. So is the opposite, namely inspiration, which amateurs are also very fond of. Putting it another way: a professional writer is someone who writes just as well when they're not inspired as when they are."

Inspiration is the reward for diligence and hard work. It doesn't magically appear when you start writing. You begin, then, on good days, inspiration shows up to lend a helping hand.

Take Barbara Kingsolver's advice.

> "I learned to produce whether I wanted to or not. It would be easy to say oh, I have writer's block, oh, I have to wait for my muse. I don't. Chain that muse to your desk and get the job done."

Perfectionism Kills

Perfectionism demands we hold out our arms while it burdens us with its unreasonable expectations. When our muscles can hold no more, perfectionism straps its heavy load over our shoulders and around our necks until we fall to the ground, dead. Any creative spark we possess is strangled by perfectionism's unbearable stress.

No one writes well under such pressure. The notion we can write a perfect first draft is absurd. On good days, we can barely write a decent sentence, let alone a full paragraph, so what makes us believe we can write an entire first draft without faults?

Unrealistic doesn't even begin to describe the insanity of this notion. The creative mind needs calm and focus to write effectively, two attributes missing when we are paralyzed by the need to be flawless.

Perfectionism burdens us with expectations we can never, ever meet. I love Don Roff's quote, because he gives me permission to write poorly.

"Writers often torture themselves trying to get the words right. Sometimes you must lower your expectations and just finish it."

Low expectations are easy to exceed. Lofty expectations are hard to meet. First drafts are the place for low expectations - the lower the better.

Done is better than perfect.

You cannot edit what you do not write.

You cannot publish what you do not complete.

I Don't Know What to Write

I don't know what to write.

An outline solves this problem. Many writers despise the outline because, well, creating an outline is hard work. We must make decisions and put order to the chaos inside our minds.

The beauty of an outline is, when it comes time to write, you always know what to write. It's there, right in front of you. Read your scene description and get on with it already.

"But I don't know what to write about," you complain.

Really? Stop lying to yourself. You know exactly what to write. Your scene description is right in front of you. Plant your butt in your chair and pound those keys. Surely to God something will come out. Then you can edit it into something readable.

Let me give you an example from my own life.

> "There's a dead body on the ground. I don't know where and I don't know why."

Impressive stuff, right? Sounds like the pathetic mewling of a guy too lazy to do his job, if you ask me.

One of the best scenes I ever wrote began with those wretched words. I frittered an entire day away, complaining that I didn't know what to write. And I only wrote those two atrocious sentences because my writing timer demanded I do something to break the back of my empty screen.

I am more powerful than a blank screen. I know this, yet I still could not get started.

All I knew about the scene was two characters needed to find a dead body on the ground. Why them? They were significant later and I needed to introduce them. Why force them to discover the dead body? I didn't know. What was their relationship with the dead guy? No clue. Why use the dead body in the first place?

Crickets.

I wracked my brain for answers. I stared at those two pitiful sentences for a long time. A very long time. I re-read my character profiles. I stared at my artistic renders of the characters. I re-read my description of who they were and what they wanted from life. Then I stared at the screen again.

Finally, the magic happened.

My fingers settled on the keyboard, then moved softly, like a pianist during the slow point of Tchaikovsky's Swan Lake.

Once the words flowed, they rushed out of me fast and furious, like the wall of water that crashes down upon a hapless desert traveler in a flash flood. I pounded my keyboard like a demon possessed and, I must tell you, what landed on the page blew my mind. It's one of the best scenes I ever wrote.

It's not the scene I planned when I created the outline.

It isn't how I intended to open the story, either. It's far better.

I had no clue where to begin when I sat down at my desk. I avoided my manuscript for the entire day until, left with no other option and a head chock full of recriminations, I clicked the start button on my writing timer and forced myself to Just Do It.

The solution is always so simple, isn't it? So why do we fight against it so hard?

Your Muse is a Tramp

Writing a book is work, hard work some days, easy work on others, but it is always work. It does not help when you sit in your easy chair and watch the rain cascade down the window as you wait for The Muse to show up. She's already here, but instead of inspiring you to greatness, she mocks and ridicules you for your sheer laziness.

Sit down at your desk and write like a demon-possessed clown holds a gun to your head and write. Your Muse won't lift a finger to help. She's far more interested in your response to the psycho clown and the soul-sucking cannon he holds to the back of your head.[5]

- ❑ Write or die.
- ❑ Make a decision.
- ❑ Follow it with action.
- ❑ Repeat.

Darynda Jones exhorts us to write every day, without fail, and scoffs at the value of The Muse.

"Real writers write. Period. No, The Muse does not come to visit everyday. She's a lazy, precocious flirt. You cannot get into the habit of being 'in the mood' to write. No writer on Earth is in the mood to write everyday, but the good ones do it anyway. They fight through their fatigue, their stress, their doubt, and they write. They get the words on the page. Period. So stop waiting for your muse. Trust me, she sleeps around."

Self-discipline to write every day, whether you feel inspired or not, gets the job done.

Waiting for The Muse to bless you with inspiration only guarantees your book will never see the light of day.

"Discipline allows magic. To be a writer is to be the very best of assassins. You do not sit down and write every day to force the Muse to show up. You get into the habit of writing every day so that when she shows up, you have the maximum chance of catching her, bashing her on the head, and squeezing every last drop out of that bitch."

— Lili St. Crow

Philip Pullman's Solution

After he ridicules writer's block as "a lot of howling nonsense," author Philip Pullman hands over the ultimate solution to every writer's malady, in whatever form he or she labels it.

"A professional writer is someone who writes just as well when they're not inspired as when they are."

The solution to writer's block in a single sentence. Beautiful.

At the core of Pullman's message is self-discipline. Professional writers write when the mood strikes and when it does not. Professional writers do what they are supposed to do, when they are supposed to do it, whether they feel like it or not.

William Faulkner reminds us about the importance of self-discipline.

"I only write when I am inspired. Fortunately, I am inspired at 9 o'clock every morning."

Without self-discipline you will never write a word, let alone finish your book.

Are you a writer? Great. Plant your butt in your chair, turn on your computer and do it.

Write every day. If you only write 500 words per day, by the end of one year, that's 182,500 words under your belt. If you take Sundays off, like I do, you'll still write 156,000 words this year. Impressive.

Sounds so easy, doesn't it?

It is.

Reward Yourself for Hitting Your Targets

I'm a big fan of rewards. If I can use a pre-existing desire to motivate me, I will.

Sour cream and onion potato chips are my favorite example. I know chips are not good for me. I don't care. I still love them. If I decreed I can never eat sour cream and onion potato chips again, I just set myself up for failure.

Banning myself from eating chips is downright stupid, so I don't bother. I turned my beloved and unhealthy snack into the reward every time I publish a book. My wife didn't think it was funny when I pointed out the massive five-pound bag of chips at Costco.

She called it cheating. I, of course, explained the deal is I get one bag of chips for every book I publish.

Sure, bag size is a loophole, but I'm a writer. I can rationalize anything.

Back to the point I attempted to make before I fell off the potato chip wagon.

I don't even try to stop eating chips forever. I make the commitment I won't eat them today. When I publish a book, I reward myself with a bag of those delicious morsels and savor every bite. Then I get back to work so I can eat another bag.

Sure, it's a gimmick, but it works. That's what matters. It works.

For me, sour cream and onion potato chips are a powerful motivator. Your mileage may vary, so find the thing you want, ideally something you know you should not do, and turn it into the reward when you meet your target word count or publish your book.

Its power comes from delayed gratification. It keeps me from living in the "Me, Now" mindset and forces me to wait for a bigger reward later. I know I will get what I want - potato chips - so "lack" mindset cannot sabotage me. I don't get to eat them today but when I hit the magic button on Amazon and publish my book, I will sit down with a big bag of chips and I won't feel bad for a millisecond.

I earned my reward and I'll enjoy every moment of it.

Yes, I understand how ridiculous this sounds. All I can assure you is, it works for me. Try it. You might find self-bribery works for you, too.

I Don't Have Time To Write, and Other Lies

Chapter 3

My First Draft Must Be Perfect

Your First Draft Should Suck

The first draft of anything is shit.

Hemingway's admonition is as true today as the day he wrote it.

The faster I write a first draft, the better. Quality is of no concern at this stage. I don't care about passive voice. I don't care about structure. I don't care about the order of my thoughts. I can fix all those issues later, but I can't fix anything until it's on the page. I must get those thoughts out of my brain, where they swirl around like grains of sand in a sandstorm, and glue them on the page so I can figure out what castles to build and where to place the turrets.

Until my first draft is complete, I ignore my Infernal Editor, another benefit of writing fast. The quicker I dump those words on the page, the less opportunity my Infernal Editor has to screw up the process. His time is not now, while I write the first draft. His time comes later, when this draft is complete. Until then, I use every method possible to keep him on the sidelines.

Writing crappy first drafts also relieves the pressure to write well. With the pressure off I write with wild abandon, knowing I can fix every issue when I reach the revision phase.

Some writers advocate editing as you go. I'm not one of them. I don't want to break the flow of my thoughts. I want to get all those words out so the story is complete.

Yes, I make notes when I find plot holes, chronological issues, character problems or whatever else I didn't think about when I constructed my outline. I highlight those issues so they are easy to find later, then I ignore them.

This is not the time to fix them. This is the time to get the words out.

Embrace this reality.

"Write freely and as rapidly as possible and throw the whole thing on paper. Never correct or rewrite until the whole thing is down. Rewrite in process is usually found to be an excuse for not going on. It also interferes with flow and rhythm which can only come from a kind of unconscious association with the material."

— John Steinbeck

The True Purpose of Your First Draft

Perfectionism is the serial killer of creativity.

Your first draft has a single purpose - to dump your ideas on the page so they can no longer rattle around inside your brain. That's all.

The outline is a process, an ever-expanding circle of fill-in-the-blanks until the story is clear and your message reads like a single, coherent thought. Your first draft is the next logical expansion of your outline.

Some of the best advice I ever received came from a screenwriting book. I don't remember the title but this author recommended I stop my characters from speaking until I'm almost finished the script.

Until your characters are fully developed and behave as real human beings would in the same circumstances, allowing them to speak just muddies the waters. It's critical to get the story and plot on the page first. Then, and only then, write their dialog.

The benefit of this approach is your characters speak with clarity and precision when you finally allow them to talk.

I used this concept with great success.

As the author promised, my characters spoke the words needed. No more, no less. This process required I understand each character in great detail, so their behavior extended naturally into their speech patterns. Dialog was the last part of the writing process, the final stage of expanding my outline, if you will.

Apply this concept to writing your book. Expand your outline over and over, in layers, until your manuscript is finished.

Writing a story, be it a novel, a screenplay, or a non-fiction book, is a process. Before you can figure out where the problems are, you must first dump words on the page and analyze what landed there. This is the only function of your first draft - to get your words on the page.

"At its root, perfectionism isn't really about a deep love of being meticulous. It's about fear. Fear of making a mistake. Fear of disappointing others. Fear of failure. Fear of success."

— Michael Law

Be fearless. Become unstoppable.

Chapter 4

I'll Remember That Great Idea

That's Such a Good Idea I Could Never Forget

"What is hell to a writer? Hell is being too busy to find the time to write or being unable to find the inspiration. Hell is suddenly finding the words but being away from your notebook or typewriter. Hell is when the verses slip through your fingers and they never return."

— R.M. Engelhardt

Let me paint you a picture. When I'm done, tell me if anything I say sounds familiar.

Exhausted after a long day, you climb into bed. You pull the blankets up around your chin and your mind roams freely as you drift off toward sleep. As you lay on the edge between wakefulness and slumber an idea strikes. It's brilliant. It's the solution to the plot problem you struggled with all day long.

There is no way you can forget an idea this good, right?

Confident in your ability to remember this perfect solution, you happily drift off to sleep. Then you wake up to this sick, nagging sensation in the pit of your stomach.

I had it. I had the solution, I just know it.

But it's gone. Worse, it never comes back.

I see you nodding your head. It sucks, losing a great idea for lack of 30 seconds of effort, doesn't it?

Put a Notepad and Pen on the Nightstand Beside Your Bed

I've lost count of how many times this scenario played out for me. I keep a note pad and a pen on the nightstand specifically for this purpose. When the idea strikes, no matter how tired I am I jump out of bed, turn on the light and write it down.

I almost never use it. It sits on the nightstand collecting dust, most of the time. But every now and then, when I need it, my notebook is there to save me.

I know I won't remember the brilliant idea floating past while my mind is relaxed. I just won't. Those repeated failures taught me one thing. When a good idea comes along, stop everything and write it down. It takes mere seconds to save the idea. Pass on this crucial moment, however, and the idea is gone forever.

Always Carry a Notebook and Pen

"Keep a notebook. Travel with it, eat with it, sleep with it. Slap into it every stray thought that flutters up into your brain. Cheap paper is less perishable than gray matter, and lead pencil markings endure longer than memory."

— Jack London

Ideas are all around us. They bombard us day in and day out, relentlessly. But only when I stop and write them down can I keep them.

An associate used to laugh whenever he saw me.

"Still carrying your notebook?" He would taunt. I just smiled and ignored him.

One day, as we discussed an issue with a client, he watched me open my notebook and jot down thoughts while I peppered our client with questions. After the meeting he asked me why.

"I must capture the important moments when they are in front of me, before the barrage of incoming information wipes them away," I answered.

He doesn't taunt me about the notebook anymore.

Chapter 5
Outlines Stifle My Creativity

I'm a Pantser, not a Plotter

If you self-identify as a Pantser (you write by the seat of your pants, not from an outline) and complain, "I don't know what to write next," you won't get any sympathy from me. Not one bit. Nobody felt sorry for me when I complained. What makes you think you're so special?

Now, before you haul out the kerosene and matches to burn me at the stake, allow me a minute to explain. I wrote my first novel by the seat of my pants. It was awful. Terrible. It wasn't the last atrocious story I ever wrote, either.

I hated the outline process.

I hated the rigidity of it. I hated how it hemmed me in. I wanted my creativity to flow, and an outline stifled my imagination. In the depths of my heart, I truly believed this nonsense.

Not only am I a slow learner, I'm also one of those folks who learns by making my own mistakes. This character flaw means I started, but did not finish, more manuscripts than I care to admit, before the pain of repeated failures forced me to rethink my process.

I finally admitted the truth. I needed structure.

I discovered, much to my delight, how easy writing was when I worked from an outline. No need to figure it out. I always know what to write next. The outline explains it all. I just need to write it. Simple.

When you decide on the contents of a particular scene, it doesn't mean you know what will happen, or what your characters will say during your scene. Even with a detailed outline, you don't know much at this point. If you're lucky, you'll know where the scene takes place, who is in the scene and you'll have a glimmer of what needs to happen to advance your story. This is light years from knowing everything or being boxed in to an unforgiving structure. It's also a far cry from sucking the creative spark out of your life.

"Writing a novel is like heading out over the open sea in a small boat. It helps if you have a plan and a course laid out."

— John Gardner

To borrow from the vernacular of 12-step programs, as a *recovering Pantser* I now plot out every book I write, both fiction and non-fiction. I even outline newspaper articles and blog posts. I write first drafts fast, as a result. It's awesome.

With fiction, I map out the entire story, plot and character arcs before I begin writing.

I won't lie. This is my least favorite part of the job.

Why? Because it's work. Bloody hard work, too. Discovering the nuances of each character is a slow process, for me. Figuring out their character arc can be even slower. This process can drag on for months (and it has) but the payoff comes when it is time to write.

I may come up with a brilliant ending and work backwards from there. I may discover a brilliant opening sequence and work my way forward until I find a satisfying conclusion. It doesn't matter which end of the story I start with, or whether I start in the middle and work my way out in both directions.

When I construct a detailed outline first, when I construct characters and take the time to learn who they are, what they want from life, and how they lie to themselves about it, I write with blinding speed.

I love it. I love pumping out a first draft of one hundred thousand words in twenty-nine days. I never came close to finishing a manuscript that fast when I wrote by the seat of my pants.

If you tell me writing an outline is too hard, I won't argue with you.

No, I will nod my head in solemn agreement. Then I will prod you to carry on. I will encourage you to spend as much time as you need to plan out every detail of your story.

When you're finished, I will encourage you to set a ridiculously short deadline to write your first draft and dare you to beat it.

"Structure is important. Know your ending before you start writing. You wouldn't just get into your car and drive without knowing where you're going. Know your most important plot points. This does not mean things won't change, but you will never get stuck."

— Peter James

Plotters vs Pantsers

"The outline is 95 percent of the book. Then I sit down and write, and that's the easy part."

— Jeffery Deaver

I'm not telling you Plotters are better than Pantsers. Not at all.

I'm telling you there's *no such thing* as Plotters or Pantsers. Every writer is both. Every writer *must* be both, to one degree or another.

Even the most fly-by-the-seat-of-their pants writer must, at some level, figure out what will happen in their story. If they don't, they'll waste enormous amounts of time figuring out how to fix the plot hole they never saw coming. With an outline, you figure this out, well in advance. You avoid creating the hole in the first place.

Structure removes the fear from writing. I'll even add "for me" to the statement, just to make you happy.

Structure removes the fear from writing, for me.

The benefits of structure outweigh its perceived horrors.

1. You always **know** what to write.
2. Because you know what to write, it's easy to **focus**.
3. An outline helps you write **faster**.
4. An outline helps you write **better**.
5. An outline makes your writing sessions **more productive**.

You don't have to figure it out. You already know where the story is headed and, if only in broad strokes, how you plan to get there.

The level of detail in your outline is almost irrelevant. What matters is that you create one, that you ask all the hard questions and make all the hard decisions first.

"I'm a great planner, so before I ever write chapter 1, I work out what happens in every chapter and who the characters are. I usually spend a year on the outline."

— Ken Follett

Some writers take a year or more to finish their outline, like Ken Follett. Others take a week or less to get their thoughts on paper before they start their first draft. What level of detail you include in your outline depends upon your personality, your need to plan your story and develop your characters.

The more time you spend writing from a carefully constructed outline, the more detailed your outlines become.

I used to write minimalist outlines, two or three lines per scene. Where the scene took place, which characters played, and where the scene turned to move the story forward. Now I write detailed notes for each scene, its characters and their goals on 4 x 6 index cards.

The more time I take to develop a detailed outline, the faster I write my first draft. It's all about speed. It's all about putting the words in my head on the page, where I can deal with them.

If my first draft is defined by speed, my editing process is defined by precision. While I can spit out an entire first draft of a hundred thousand words in a month, I'll spend six months or more refining those words into a manuscript worthy of publication.

But I can't refine words if they aren't on the page. I must complete the first draft, well, first.

Done is better than perfect. I cannot publish what I do not complete.

I make a game of writing first drafts, too, with their own special set of rewards. I count the total number of scenes in my story. I divide the it by the days remaining until my deadline. If the result is 3.5 scenes per day, then I challenge myself to write 4 scenes per day, every day. My goal is to cut as many days from my first draft as possible.

A deadline isn't there to be met. It's there to be beat.

Every day I carve from my first draft is one more day I can devote to editing. This is where I take all my jumbled thoughts, cut them into pieces and shuffle them around until a polished manuscript with a cohesive story and compelling characters falls out the other end.

Then I repeat the process after feedback from beta readers. I love it, despite all the hard work.

I refuse to release a manuscript into the world until it reflects the best work I am capable of today.

Do I believe my work is perfect? No.

It is, however, the best manuscript I can deliver with the skills I possess today.

I'll hate it tomorrow. Of course, I'll hate it tomorrow. By then I'll know more. My skills will be honed a little sharper, my eye for flaws a little clearer.

I will always find problems with what I wrote yesterday. If I worried about that, I would never publish a word.

Done is better than perfect and published is better than a manuscript rotting on my hard drive.

I Don't Have Time To Write, and Other Lies

Chapter 6

I Don't Need A Professional Editor

My Mother/Brother/Friend Can Edit My Book

I'll just edit it myself. I'm a good writer. It will be fine.

To paraphrase the old lawyer saying, a writer who is his own editor has a fool for a client.

Any writer who lies to him or herself this way needs to face reality. You, the writer, are too close to the subject matter to deal with your manuscript objectively.

The same is true of the writer who believes a family member or friend can edit their work. Like the writer, family members and friends are far too close to you to make the hard choices required. Worse, unless they are English professors, they won't see your plot holes either.

While the characters are crystal clear in your mind, does your vision of them translate to the page? This is not a question the writer can answer dispassionately. An editor can help you resolve these issues long before you dig yourself into a hole you cannot climb out of, both emotionally and financially.

I take no issue with you lying to yourself about every other subject in this book, so long as you don't lie to yourself here. This is where I draw my line in the sand. This is where you, the author, must be brutally honest with yourself.

It is hard enough to earn a reputation as an author to be trusted. Don't toss it away before you even begin.

If you believe your mother, brother or best friend can edit your book, you're wrong. Unless one of these lovely people knows how to write well and understands the skills an editor brings to the table, they are the wrong choice.

An editor brings many skills to the table, including objectivity.

It's impossible for your family or friends to give you an unbiased opinion. They don't want to hurt your feelings. They will hesitate to tell you the truth.

An editor must point out the cold, hard facts and force the writer to hear them.

If you write fiction, you probably require two different types of editor - a story editor and a manuscript editor.

The story editor, oddly enough, deals with story issues.

Does your plot work? Does it flow effectively? Is it well-paced? Does your theme weave through every scene of your book? Are your characters vibrant and real, or cardboard cutouts readers will toss aside before the end of page three? What pieces don't fit? What essential elements are missing?

The manuscript editor deals with writing craft issues.

Are there spelling errors? Do you use words in their proper context? Does your dialog sound realistic, or is it flat and predictable, like your characters? What words, sentences or entire paragraphs can you cut and still retain your message? Where must you strengthen the tone and cohesiveness of your story? What cliché little darlings do you hang on to? Your editor will tell you what you already know. Kill them. Kill them all.

Remember, your story must sing to your reader, and even the best writers alive today rely on editors to polish their manuscripts to the crescendo required to meet reader expectations and maintain their author reputation.

There's a lesson in there somewhere, I'm sure.

Chapter 7

I'm Not Talented Enough To Be A Writer

God Gave You Talent

You are blessed. Your ability to craft words into beautiful thoughts is a calling, a gift from God.

What you do with the talent God gave you is up to you.

Write every day. Hone the talent God gave you into a mighty skill, then wield your skill with integrity and grace.

There is one major difference between successful authors and the majority of writers. Successful authors worked hard to develop whatever raw talent God gave them into the mighty skill readers drool over. Readers (and fellow writers) only see the finished product, the result of long years of practice and countless hours of editing.

Name the famous author of your choice. I guarantee they were terrible writers when they first started.

Writing is a job and, as with any job, you must show up every day, on time and do the work. It's precisely this simple and this hard.

I leave you with these wise words from William Faulkner. Ignore them at your peril.

"Don't be a writer; be writing."

One Last Thing!

First, thank you for reading this book!

If you enjoyed this book and found it informative (and even if you did not) I would be grateful if you would post an honest review on Amazon and/or Goodreads. Every review helps this book find more readers, the lifeblood of any author.

http://ChristopherDiArmani.net/review-lies-amazon

http://ChristopherDiArmani.net/review-lies-goodreads

Your support in the form of an honest review really does make a difference. Reviews help authors sell more books and I read every one as part of my efforts to make my books even better.

I would also be grateful if you shared a link to this book on your social media accounts.

If, for some reason, you did not like this book or didn't get what you expected out of it please tell me directly. I will use your constructive criticism to fix any flaws in my book so it better meets your expectations. Please contact me here:

https://ChristopherDiArmani.net/Contact

Thank you so much for your support, feedback and your honest reviews.

Sincerely,

Christopher di Armani

Author Extraordinare

http://ChristopherDiArmani.net/Books

About Christopher di Armani

"Author Extraordinaire"

Christopher di Armani is an Amazon bestselling author and the creator of Author Success Foundations.

This 7-book series teaches authors at any level how to develop the mindset, daily routines and work habits necessary to unleash their creativity and get their books published.

He has published 16 books and produced 4 documentary films on topics ranging from the craft of writing to civil liberties and politics.

Download your free introduction to the Author Success Foundations series at

https://ChristopherDiArmani.net/AuthorSuccessFoundations

Books by Christopher

Awaken Your Author Mindset: Finish Writing Your Book Fast (Author Success Foundations 1)

https://ChristopherDiArmani.net/author-mindset

https://ChristopherDiArmani.net/author-mindset-workbook

Learn how to develop your bullet-proof Author Mindset and create a system guaranteed to deliver success and to build the habits required to work this system every single day.

The choice is yours. If you continue to do what you've always done you'll just get what you already have, an unfinished manuscript and all the disappointment, discarded dreams and self-loathing you can handle.

You will never finish your book.

Now, imagine the possible…

Allow me to be your guide to help you construct a mindset, a solid foundation to complete your manuscript so published becomes, not just possible, but inevitable. This is the power of the Author Mindset.

Design Your Morning Routine: Jump-Start Your Writing Success (Author Success Foundations Book 2)

https://ChristopherDiArmani.net/morning-routine

https://ChristopherDiArmani.net/morning-routine-workbook

There is no magic to writing a book. None. You take action, every single day, until your book is finished. You plan, schedule and execute the plan. You write.

If you are serious about finishing your manuscript, grab your notebook, a pen, and a cup of your favorite beverage, and join me at the kitchen table. We'll chat about habits, willpower and self-discipline. We'll discuss how the mind functions, what makes a habit stick, and how our willpower fades throughout the day. We'll talk about concrete steps to improve your self-discipline.

Then I'll ask you to complete a series of exercises. These exercises reveal, at a deep level, what's important to you - what you value most in life. This clarity of purpose allows you to create a morning routine designed to jump-start your daily writing output.

Author Focus: Develop Your Author Vision Statement and Laser-Focus Your Writing Career (Author Success Foundations Book 3)

https://ChristopherDiArmani.net/author-focus

https://ChristopherDiArmani.net/author-focus-workbook

Writing is easy. Finishing your book is easy, too.

Focus. Be diligent. Apply self-discipline and determination.

You already possess these qualities. This book would not appeal to you if you didn't.

Your author vision statement is an extraordinary targeting mechanism to guide you to your ultimate destination - the end of Publication Highway.

The exercises ahead serve one purpose - to focus your mind on what you value most - your published book.

Join me and map your personal journey down Publication Highway. Discover what you value most, not just in writing, but in your entire life.

Isn't your ideal future worth the time?

Prolific Author: The Step-by-Step Guide to Write More Words in Less Time and Finish Your Book Fast (Author Success Foundations 4)

https://ChristopherDiArmani.net/prolific-author

https://ChristopherDiArmani.net/prolific-author-workbook

The key to unlock your drive to succeed is knowing why you write. When you understand how your desire to write fulfills your core needs, you transform writing from a chore to be dreaded into the vision you were born to fulfill. Time set aside to write becomes as critical to your life as the food you eat and the water you drink.

If we believe success does not matter, neither does the road we travel to get there.

Success matters. The road you travel to achieve success matters more.

Your daily writing routine is the last piece of the puzzle to build a life focused on accomplishing your goal - a finished and published book.

Done is Better than Perfect: 7 Keys to Finish Writing Your Book Fast (Author Success Foundations 5)

https://ChristopherDiArmani.net/done-better-perfect

Give Up Your Perfectionism and Publish Your Book

The three fundamental truths of writing are:

1. Your book will never be perfect.
2. You cannot publish what you do not complete.
3. Done is better than perfect.

Learn how to finish your book easier, faster and better than you ever thought possible when you apply the Seven Keys of Writing Success.

Become Unstoppable: 7 Habits of Highly Successful Authors (Author Success Foundations Book 6)

https://ChristopherDiArmani.net/become-unstoppable

Success leaves clues.

Figure out what successful authors did to advance their careers, then do what they did. It's the most effective course of action. Simple concept, but we must do the work. You know, the hard part.

In the pages ahead I discuss how each habit works, as well as the lies we tell ourselves to rationalize our lack of forward progress. Finally, I shine the light of truth on the lies we tell ourselves and watch as they scurry away like little cockroaches.

Apply these principles to your life and you'll achieve their success. It's inevitable. All it takes is a pinch of perseverance, a dash of focus, and two cups of hard work.

I Don't Have Time To Write And Other Lies Writers Tell Themselves (Author Success Foundations Book 7)

https://ChristopherDiArmani.net/no-time-to-write

Stop Lying To Yourself.

In this installment of the Author Success Foundations series, I dissect seven lies writers tell ourselves and shine the light of truth upon each one.

Every falsehood obscures a truth we refuse to confront. The job of a writer, any writer, is to face our fears head on, protected by the body armor of honesty and integrity. Only then does the brilliance we etch on the page shine bright for the world to see.

Each delusion corrodes holes in our armor, holes the insidious demons of worry, self-doubt, procrastination and perfectionism slip through to poison us.

The Author Success Foundations series provides the tools and materials to patch those holes, to reinforce and strengthen our armor. The day of battle is here, and we must march ever forward. If we stop, even for a moment, our words shrink under the oppressive heat of our fears and we fail.

Step inside. Face your fears. Show these pathetic demons you cannot be cowed. Own your internal dialog and reshape it into a powerful engine, then use that power to drive down Publication Highway.

The Simple 3-Step Secret to Slaughter Writer's Block And Vanquish it Forever

https://ChristopherDiArmani.net/Writers-Block-Book

There is no more perfect Hell than one where I cannot write. You know that terror, too, don't you? That sense your last remaining creative spark abandoned you some time back. It's sickening.

Let me show you how to extricate yourself from that "perfect Hell" permanently.

TOP SECRET - Inspiration, Motivation and Encouragement - 701 Essential Quotes for Writers

https://ChristopherDiArmani.net/Top-Secret-Quotes

This compilation of 701 quotes delivers inspiration, motivation and encouragement on 39 aspects of writing and the writing life.

You will discover quotes to make you laugh and quotes to make you cry. Some are familiar, like old friends. Others you will meet for the first time. All have a common theme: The Writing Life.

When you need it most, you will find words of encouragement here.

Filming Police is Legal - How to Hold Police Accountable While Staying Out of Jail

I write about police issues regularly. I highlight good cops when I can, but I focus on the problems in our police forces with honesty, integrity and abuse. Every time news breaks about police seizing another citizen's camera or cell phone I receive the same question.

Christopher, is it legal to film police?

The unequivocal answer is a court-affirmed YES. It is legal to film police in every state in the United States of America and in every single province and territory of Canada. That YES comes with specific caveats for the audio portion of a recording depending upon your jurisdiction, and it is critical you know those caveats.

The purpose of this book is to educate mere citizens and police forces alike about the legality of the right of citizens to film police, along with an examination of the legal history supporting our legal right to do so.

https://ChristopherDiArmani.net/Filming-Police

Justin Trudeau - 47 Character-Revealing Quotes from Canada's 23rd Prime Minister and What They Mean for You

On October 19, 2015 Canadians elected their 23rd Prime Minister based on good looks, nice hair and a famous name.

They voted for style over substance.

Our 23rd Prime Minister's entire leadership experience consisted of teaching snowboarding lessons and high school drama. His management experience consisted of administering his trust fund and his ego.

Not a single thought was given to what he stood for, what his party stood for, or what he would actually do once elected to the highest office in the land. That bothered me. That bothered me so much I began to research his much-publicized missteps and that in turn revealed a disturbing pattern within Trudeau's numerous faux pas. That pattern is the focus of this book.

https://ChristopherDiArmani.net/Justin-Trudeau-Book-1

From Refugee to Cabinet Minister: Maryam Monsef's Meteoric Rise to Power and her Spectacular Fall From Grace

Maryam Monsef is the ultimate immigrant success story. She could not speak English when she arrived in Canada at age eleven. Two decades later she became Canada's first Muslim Cabinet Minister.

Maryam Monsef's story begins with her mother, a young Afghan widow who fled Afghanistan for Canada with her three young daughters in 1995. That widow spoke English but her three daughters did not. They brought something far more valuable to Canada: the unshakeable belief they could accomplish anything they wanted, so long as they worked hard.

It's no accident her belief in herself led Maryam Monsef to a Cabinet post. She worked hard to learn English and graduated from Trent University, an impossible accomplishment in her native Afghanistan.

Maryam Monsef became the unwitting scapegoat for Trudeau's broken promise on electoral reform, a promise he knew he would break by May 2016. Her birthplace controversy, her attempts to discredit and insult her electoral reform committee, combined with the Prime Minister's betrayal of her trust, sounded the death knell of her political career.

This, then, is the story of one young woman's meteoric rise to political power. It is also the story of that young woman's undoing at the hands of a narcissistic and self-serving celebrity feminist, Justin Trudeau.

https://ChristopherDiArmani.net/Maryam-Monsef-Book

Endnotes

1.   Wikipedia contributors. (2018, March 6). Writer's block. In Wikipedia, The Free Encyclopedia. Retrieved 16:18, March 15, 2018, from https://en.wikipedia.org/w/index.php?title=Writer%27s_block&oldid=829091802
2.   "writer's block." In Merriam-Webster.com. Retrieved March 15, 2018, from https://www.merriam-webster.com/dictionary/writer%27s%20block
3.   writer's block. (n.d.). Dictionary.com Unabridged. Retrieved March 15, 2018 from Dictionary.com website http://www.dictionary.com/browse/writer-s-block
4.   writer's block. (n.d.). UrbanDictionary.com. Retrieved March 15, 2018 from UrbanDictionary.com website https://www.urbandictionary.com/define.php?term=writer%27s+block
5.   "Write Like There's No Tomorrow" by Christopher di Armani. https://www.renderosity.com/mod/gallery/write-like-theres-no-tomorrow/2734284/?p

www.ingramcontent.com/pod-product-compliance
Lightning Source LLC
Chambersburg PA
CBHW070858050426
42453CB00012B/2262